Into the Shallows

Heather Gatley

For Anne

Cover Photograph, Heather Gatley

The Corner

When you remember us,
pause at this unremarkable corner,
a small concrete lay-by chained off,
and I, walking inside the chains
for as long as possible,
looking over at the low house
or the strange shop that may not be a shop,
and the large boulder garden
with its Chinese characters that we cannot yet read.
It is a sunny day, as many were,
hot under the Taiwan sky.
We were lonely, we were grateful.
We were on the edge of life.
You were kind.
We had our histories and they were history.
We still had our companions,
but most of all,
we had each other.
And that corner is the place
where we shall always be walking,
just about to turn into the stream of life,
but really, invisible.

Catching Colours with Susan

On perfect days, 27 degrees,
not too much sun,
a taxi up the preposterous mountain
to the house of Sahar.
Beautiful coloured scarves,
tunics, cloth and jewels
and a turtle in his tank
watching the joy.
From the window,
the quiet jungle, not a breath of wind,
no earthquake or typhoon,
only enormous butterflies,
stately, in slow motion.
And a taxi down to Sogo,
cosmetics and lunch,
and stories of old, old days with you.
And yet there were no better days than these,
nothing was asked of us,
and everything.
But giving comes easy here,
because you are with me,
catching the colours of memory.
This day in Tianmu.

Dragon Smoke

When I am old
with Hello Kitty clips
in my dragon-smoke hair,
I shall put my poems into books,
madden my children with all my thoughts,
and watch the kids go to school in prison buses.
I shall trip up and down Sulphur Creek, counting turtles,
pretend to learn Chinese,
waste my days playing word games,
or watching unsuitable films.
I'll be alone in this conspiracy of
elemental days where you strip away the years
and find out who you are inside,
the kernel you had to coat in layers to survive:
writer of poems
singer alone
drawer of roses in the morning
climber of trees
sitter amongst dunes
painter of palms.
I'll ask, are the bulbs coming up in your garden
as we prepare to go down into the darkness
all of us, all of us?
Bring the silence of the sea,
graveyard and Celtic cross.

Free

I was free,
so I ran in the wind.
I felt free,
so I ran for my life.
I was free!
I ran in the wind,
in the far, far south,
by the deep blue sea.
I was free.

I was possessed,
and so were we,
so we ran
in the wind on Solsbury hill,
for we were free.

When I'm free,
look for me,
for I run in the wind,
on the hills,
by the sea,
in the air.
Free

Old Age

Old age came rushing in
with death and defibrillation,
the pavement crushing your head,
leaving the scars to carry on.

When you look back you know:
this was the moment,
this was the day,
and each morning
it becomes easier to say:

I am old now, I am old,
how can I plan to keep out the cold?
How can I keep my feet on the ground,
hoping more days will come around?

Chinese by numbers

Very quickly now, the numbers are leaving me.
I see a day when I'm left with lonely yi,
and though good things come in pairs,
I was ever unsure on pronouncing er.
Lucky San hung around wistfully,
but so did suh, death's heavy knell.
Jui, good old Joe, longevity,
he was first to go,
and I had to search for him.
Then it was Mr. Wu. Number five.
Good luck or bad luck?
What use years of classes
if I can't even keep the numbers alive,
and their strange night time shapes escape?

A tree as lovely as a poem

Of your constant Renaissance
and perfect green leaves,
I had so much to say.
The golden rod of tiny blossom,
cone-like and so comely,
twice a year.
And the heart-shaped seed cases,
like rusting bougainvillea,
first silver, then burnished copper.
I wanted to praise you
and to know your name,
and then I found out
it was Flame Gold Rain.
And there was no need of this poem

Redeem the Time

So much left undone and the house unsold,
the bicycle hangs rusting from the beam.
Redeem, redeem the time you put on hold.

Because you walked away in days of old,
the fight or flight of something in a dream,
so much left undone and the house unsold.

Go back, you'll only find a breath of mould,
though honeyed are the memories, it seems.
Redeem, redeem the time you put on hold.

The grasses of midsummer are blown cold,
the waters of the bay no longer teem.
So much left undone and the house unsold.

You ran your heedless ways, the story's told,
the scattered stones of churchyards seem to gleam.
Redeem, redeem the time you put on hold.

And since a Chinese box collapsed and closed,
imagination must provide the theme.
So much left undone and the house unsold.
Redeem, redeem, the time you put on hold.

Desultory Tamsui

If you go, go alone,
take the walk past counters
of aluminium teapots
foot massage chairs
all the little corner shops.
Try not to trip on the stones
or fall as a moped races the corner.
Keep masked and ready.
Cross at the lights.
Ignore the people,
they are not going your way.
The sky is clear
it's only you today.
The carriage, majestic trees
steep smoking hills,
ignore all these.
When the mangroves appear,
look through, imagine frogs.
The sea approaches under Bali mountain.
Today there is a blue swell
entering the mouth of the freshwater port
where the tall gantries face China.
The white eyes of blue, green and red sampans,
line up steadily under lamps,
each one a perch for a seagull.
Disembark in the desultory peace,
a wander along the promenade.
Alone. This day. Tamsui.
Fresh air and blue sea.

Ms Yang

She comes in upright, dark haired,
pretty as a kitten.
I beckon her to the room,
the ironing board piled with clothes:
the summer dresses I shall weep over,
the failed shoes, some new.
She is petite and young,
has hung out of thirteenth floor windows
dressed in black,
nimble as a ninja.
Unafraid on her moped,
withdrawing mops and brooms
from the compact seat
like Mary Poppins,
depositing her pink helmet,
she arrives with a laden bag,
changes into athletic gear,
and cleans my house
while I sit here.
Ms. Yang:
My helper of four years.

Small Dog. Black Car

Small dog, oh please don't bark at evening,
it echoes into the cavern that is my soul
in the late afternoon when the light is low.

Black car please don't follow me so slow,
snapping at my heels as though you know
that I am here, and so alone.

Oh where is the help for this soul despair?
these grey tiled blocks loom down and stare.

I smell the food I cannot eat,
hear voices I don't understand,
see the children and dogs in their prams.

I don't even know where else I would go.
All the cities are ruined for me.
The temple incense tells me so.

Dogs Don't Care

When you're only writing doggerel
And are slouching in a chair
Annoyed about a vaccine
And the colour of your hair
When you think the world is vile now
And you miss the country fair
Just grab the nearest canine
Remember, dogs don't care!

When your daughter's trapped in Russia
And your friend's chased by a bear
And you're sitting locked inside
Because go out you do not dare
And you've been marooned in Taiwan
For much more than a year
Just grab hold of that chihuahua
Because dogs don't care.

If the outlook is impossible
Then retire to your lair
And recall it's not so great
Over in Weston-Super-Mare
Just put it in perspective
Find a friend with whom to share
This comforting prognosis
That dogs don't care!

Poem from a lazy cat

Is it ok that most days
I only manage the achievements
of a cat?
I roll from bed early
after ten hours there,
seeking a morsel,
there is no need to prepare:
the integral beauty of the golden kiwi.
I read some mails,
check on Facebook,
sort out the washing up
(three cups),
take a shower and a few stretches,
cat stretches,
play a word game,
scroll the doom of news,
then dash from shade to shade for half an hour,
to retire once more to the bed,
to cower from heat,
with the old pressures beating in:
You ought to work.
Work, damn you!
But I slink away to pretend,
to meditate and relax.
How much more relaxed can I be?
The achievements of a cat,
without even a bird,
without grace and skill,
waiting with time to kill.

Awakenings

The depth of stars is in my eye.
I crawl, a tiny mite, leaving my trail.
Onward we go, without a sail.
Please don't force me into churches grey,
replete with the mourners of yesterday.
I cannot bear the mildewed aisles,
the bonnets, pews, the priests of guile.
Sometimes this Earth, so stale and cruel,
makes me look up but shiver too.
Sometimes I see the stair unfold.
But other days I'm not so bold.
Soft comes the spring,
sweet grows the air,
awakenings are hard to bear.

Time Wasted

Death happens to other people,
who squander time,
galloping forward,
or slumbering in a rut,
or scrambling out of it,
until the day someone doesn't come home,
or a scan reveals a tumour,
or a childhood friend takes that mysterious journey
without even telling.
Over that golden thread of sixty,
the world no longer means it.
Retire to a chair, unaware of who stands,
in shadow under the pelmet,
or at the goalpost of imagined aims.
Just by degrees, edge toward
that plunging cliff of culling.
And then all the birds are to be envied,
all the struggling youngsters pushing prams,
with dark rings under their eyes,
all the families squabbling on holidays,
reflections of thrown away yesterdays.
Death happens to other people,
unaware of the great crowd
pushing towards the narrow hall,
into the corridor just off the waiting room,
hoping a doctor had the answer.
Time wasted. Time squandered.
Time lost in that world you once wandered.

Istanbul 1981

A childish traveller, I.
Who can poeticise this place?
For it possesses you, not the other way around.
Long hours, the trundling train –
passengers stepping off
to pick plums from laden trees.
Fields of reaping peasants,
pitchforks, haystacks and carts.
Golden Horn, miniature ships.
A carpet of cats.
Coffee sellers, brass urns on their backs.
A solitude in the flowing crowd of Galata.
Filigree wooden balconies, spindled minarets.
Here may be something close to your real self,
pulling East and West.
A morning of gold dust,
red with pomegranate.
Far away shouts and distant memory.
Almost a child,
she stands at the station,
a tasselled scarf,
green overalls, yellow framed rucksack.
Istanbul. 1981.

Travelling Backwards

I've never minded it,
the spires receding in a blur of trees,
rooftops of suburbia, other lives
flying forward into their own futures.
Away they go, familiar old platforms,
windows into the deep mine of my years.
Some say such as this disorients them,
upsets their order, into dizziness,
but I revel in the chestnut candles,
the river banks peopled by wild swimmers,
which I used to merely call swimming.
The world is more frantic and crowded now,
so, happily speeding away from it,
I may reach a quieter memory:
canal, aqueduct, road and rail aligned,
the deep cutting heavy with the summer,
keeping memories of what was my time.
My youth, my foolishness, my delusions,
all hang in the steamy rain, leaves new sprung,
waving as I sit, glimpsing a moment,
something that stayed just there fifty years gone.
Travelling backwards now, for new memories
which I'll hang on this long chain of my past,
shimmering in yellow spring laburnum,
something sweet and poignant as foolish youth.
I shan't remember the faltering steps,
panicked fidgeting of the elderly.
Oh no, the backward journey will go fast
in fog, for such a one as I am now.
I've never minded travelling backwards.

One Road

By glacial valleys and ribbed hills,
bow lakes and river meanders,
empty expanse bears just one road.
Spiteful, narrow, fierce it wanders,
carved by the bones whose souls withdrew.
No trundling carriage passes through,
this road assuredly built for you.
No lay-by grants a soft respite,
no picnic table will invite,
relentlessly it carves out the night.

O please slow down, let me rest a while!
Let me just step out and over that stile.
On goes the cruel and deadly road,
invisible bearer of your soul.

For Sue and Phil

On your wedding day
they put up a white umbrella
outside the chapel in the Welsh rain.
But though it was held by the chauffeur
really, it was you.
Over the shining black hair and eyes
of the boy next door
who lost his mother too young,
your summer soul poured light.
Through the hail and grey winters
along the wild shores of Gower
you sheltered your daughters
and your dear lover
under your white umbrella.

Cup Full

You came to visit one year on
widowed by the boy you knew
when we were young.
How do you manage to go on?
But there you are, as bright as day
the cup still full as always.
We chat and walk and openly,
"It's one year now," you say clearly.
Only later for a cup of tea
does he appear in our company.
I set the cups, not for us three,
but for a fourth, inadvertently.
I, watching you survive a thing of fear
set out the cup for your lost dear.

The Wreckage

"I'll tell you a Daisy story,"
said the old man in his second year of widowhood,
and you could see it on his face:
the descent from disbelief complete.
I helped him finish his story, for it was ravaged:
bare bones like the black spars of the wreck in the bay,
hull sunk deep in the century.
"She used to come every Sunday,
the only day Mags drank tea instead of coffee.
Then she would read your tea leaves:
'Be careful of Handel, your husband,'
she said once, but his heart failed anyway,
almost the next day, along the cruel railway."
I thirst now for the stories that I know by heart.
Withdrawn from the scene,
the sea mists cover my words,
and new hills speak little to me,
seeming like iron scales loaded one on one,
rising into huge skies,
waiting for snows.
There is a tussle now of loyalty,
as I left the sea for my husband.
'Be careful of Handel,' said Daisy.
"I'll tell you a story," said the old man.
But oh those broken spars!
The Wreckage of longings.

Sunspot

Ah the old railway sleeper,
no need of a carven bench.
We would sit in that sunspot
admiring the vegetables.
What more is needed?
Just loved ones together in the sun,
up against the old wall,
smiling into the camera
while the pea rows waved
and the poppies nodded.

Oblivion

The water slid in like glass on a tray,
and a lone white bird flew by on its way.
The mirror was streaked in lines of sharp light,
reflecting promising pearls, end of night.

A greyness dispersing to hopeful blue,
and the colours of houses, pastel hue.
The trees held their arms waving catkin bells,
unheard, the spring was astir in the dells.

Now silence is king and tranquil and grey,
small birds flit unheard above the cold bay.
There's no one to see and nothing to say.
Shadows sink into the waters all day.

A white bird banks and screeches all forlorn,
liquid glass speeds up as it slides to town.
No invader, fisherman, trawler, sail
no triremes, galleons, cutters avail,
Yachtsman, coracle, ketch, oarsman and yawl,
long sailed on, to oblivion. All.

Coffee

The efficacy of coffee is unknown,
though it will probably fuck us pretty soon,
like the cigarettes ignorant parents smoked,
there are many certain roads towards our doom.

The asteroids swarm around our lonely heads
and deserts heat and forests furnace hold,
we edge by moments to our destined beds,
this tragedy was long ago foretold.

Drink water, beer or Coca Cola dear,
it makes no difference as it all turns out.
Run marathons or recline in easy chair,
nothing can hold you from the deathly rout.

Round and round the wagon we all run,
demon pitch forks ranged against our try
to deny above our feckless deeds undone,
we fall back helpless, with a piteous cry.

Eat, drink and be merry while you all still can,
the dancer's bones crack to the fiddler's tune,
the bells of time relentlessly toll your span,
there's really only one road to your doom.

Cake Orlandesque

On the auspicious occasion of cutting the cake,
it falls to me now that a speech I must make.
And finding ourselves in the Land of our Fathers,
it seems only right to convey it in bad verse.
For this is the old home of four generations
of Davies's born on this beautiful turf.
There was Great Grandad Benji, a bit of a villain,
and Grandad of mine whose name it was Evan.
But fondest of all of music and poetry,
was my father Orlando who loved to compose it.
I'm sure he is watching along with his Mam,
my grandmother Daisy, my Nanna, my Gran.
She would be delighted to see her old home
with all of you gathered to bless the Union,
of Grisha and Jane, with all that is merry,
I wish you much joy in your new life in ferry!

Love you both!
Cheers!
13th August, 2022

The Curse

Walk with me,
for the shadows of the morning are on the hill,
and the blossoms of springtime are fixed and still.
Walk with me while we still can,
up the steep hill to the old church,
to sit above the graves and feel assured
that to sleep is safe in this soft corner,
while the peacock butterfly rests on stone,
celtic crosses and sailor's anchors,
for those called home.
Let us sit in silence above the sea,
or the golden sandbanks of the sun,
or the swishing of the oak,
watched only by the bar-eyed goat,
dumb creatures all, except,
to be aware of that final call,
is our curse. That is all.

Wendy Bancroft

Pause a while by this simple cross,
for she was a friend,
an enemy to no one,
and left too soon.
Lately she worshipped here,
now she rests
and the sands are lit
in snaking silver
laid out like the curls
on the neck of a Greek maid
or the beaten gold collar
of an Egyptian pharaoh.
And she is as old
and as young as they were.

Go Out!

Look! Midsummer shadows are upon the hill,
and there is not enough time to get your fill!
The laden blossom is lighter now,
thread bare amongst new leaves of May,
and there is not enough time to enjoy the day.
Faint blue the sky, tide running away.
Go out, go out! Go out and play!
I'll go up hills, I'll fight my way,
it's taking longer every day,
the aching knee, the shortening breath,
come fairy child, come, come away!
The dainty aspens flutter and dance,
their silver sides say summer will pass.
The day your mother was lain down,
her favourite month was all around,
just bees and garden and her chair,
before her time ran out down here.
Look! Midsummer shadows are on the hill,
and there is not enough time to get your fill.

Heatwave

It's the kind of day that makes you plan for a chocolate
biscuit.
How can this estuary remain so pearly grey?
I encounter dogman at the archway,
he of the fingerless black leather gloves,
with studs,
the army issue waistcoat plastered in badges,
pointy-bearded, catweazle-thin, and toothless.
- I've had 18 dogs at a time
they don't give any trouble
they know who's in charge.-

There's a heatwave everywhere;
so is that rain?
You need an oscar in raised spirits in this place,
and perhaps that is all we are,
the DNA wandered out of the churchyard,
or is it the sandbanks that send the menfolk crazy,
the tiny cottage rooms filled with projects:
spare planks
old dinghies
ropes and ties
cockle-sieves,
spilling across the road
where trailers, boats and extra cars reside?
See the kitchen, her only real space,
no wonder it takes more than a smile to crack her face.

And here's Captain Pugwash's hardly-legal place.
There's no end to the mythologising here,
I can pour legends of nothingness into your ear.
But hark, the Bhangra music!
see the septuagenarian dance,
a garlanded tuk-tuk and a widower's glance:
- I'll be full-on crazy - his bent frame says
undaunted on the foreshore.
- Anyone want a ride?
Tuk Tuk for hire.-
No heatwave here
but this soul is still on fire!

Cwmfrwdd.

A place pleasingly bereft of vowels,
and yet surely meaning comfort,
or even come forth.
There, one day, we left the bus
having no car right then,
and walked the path
alive with meadowsweet,
the smell of memory
and summer.
There, on the corner,
a bungalow, which I abhor
yet called me to its lonely door,
said: come forth and live in me,
and I shall always offer
summer lanes of waving grass,
warmth and memory of youth.
You will not need to leave.
Cwmfrwdd.

Autumn

She bares her chest like a Victorian lady
at a private soirée.
The morning light picks out her colours,
frilled green and flouncing.
Ochre and yellow, her necklace a hedgerow,
laden with rose-hips, hawthorn berries.
A navy tide pulling fast away
at a yoghurt pot of a winsome boat,
bobbing white under the clouded sun
pointing gamely out to sea now
held close by the tiny red buoy,
and all the little houses under green trees
lining the white sanded shore
until your heart wants to break.

The Stable Door

One thing:
a wooden stable door
open to the warm morning sun
which I lean out peacefully from.
A garden full of flowers,
my home, all spruced and, battened down
from winter storm, or summer flood,
so warm and safe with you, my one.
But even when I picture this,
the door looks shut and we are gone.

Wilf who knots his handkerchief

Now I am that person,
she in a coat and hat with pin,
big bosomed and carrying a carpet bag,
walking arm in arm with him.
Or Auntie Blanche, Una or Grace.
Now I'm old enough to imagine they lived,
not introspective selfish and young,
unable to picture where I had come from.
I am the eye in the crowd on the beach,
looking up to the promenade or the pier.
I sit wrapped up on a striped deck chair,
with Wilf who knots his handkerchief.
I carry a flag in a brass band parade,
Abide With Me, be not afraid.
These were my parents' yesterdays,
their childhoods I could not conceive,
but in my old age, as they had theirs
the black and white people spring to life:
Past, Present, Future, all seem one,
only blindness to it is for the young.

Old Man's Beard

When I was a small child just starting school,
winter meant snivelling in bus stop queues,
wiping our noses on cold gabardine.
The teachers would take us on nature walks,
ragged line stumbling in tussocky grass.
Under high frosty hedges all so brown,
they would pause and talk of the hips and haws,
and old man's beard which I less understood.

Today the frost came in with a white fog
which took its time to suggest it might lift,
rising from the tangled unkempt garden
where fat brown sparrows were hoping for seed.
I thought about those trying nature walks,
considering what old man's beard might mean.

Breakfast with Fiona

Early we walked out to your wide garden,
brought fresh milk in an honest china jug
to a trestle table close to the fence,
unctuously watched by a lounging pig.
The raspberries were ripe on your bushes
and the English strawberries lush and sweet,
the sun and breeze touched the rustling leaves
and the neighbour's horse stood contentedly,
his companion sheep comfortingly by.
Summer, under light blue sky in England.
The dale where your home nestles, golden fields,
wild flowers, winding paths and woodland walks,
your welcome smile, calm complexion and tone.
For a moment, I breathed the lost air of home.

Glastonbury

You are Carol King and Carly Simon,
a grandad shirt and pair of coloured loons,
floppy hat, fringed and braided shoulder bag,
long hair, Laura Ashley skirts and smock shirts.
You are vinyl albums, roaches and joints,
a pint of cider and a country pub,
moped rides and walks by the old canal,
candle laden grandeur of chestnut trees.

Green and white apple blossom memory,
the hippie town of old Glastonbury.
A grey arched doorway to eternity,
a tarot priestess gown of imagery.
Sinister horror of the hangman's noose,
reminder of a king's monstrosity.

Lost Century

Simnel cake and Easter Bonnets,
Whit weddings and white gloves,
the old guard withdrew,
their bear skins and salutes,
their sentry boxes and attention
into the distant parade of history,
offspring of arrows that landed
from distant Agincourt to Waterloo.

Left behind, mourning isn't our thing,
but still, there is a vertigo.
We fall a little with them,
leaving with a lost century,
the revered pillars of another wisdom,
taken to the chapel tomb.

House Hunting

The plush red carpets
and bespoke wood kitchen,
glasses hanging as in a saloon,
terraced garden ending in moors,
rhododendron and peonie,
summers with the family,
gone now.This empty nest,
testimony to a lifetime of trying.

Here's a serial killer:
lumberjack shirt and peaked cap,
grinning lugubriously with his knife:
-     Shall I show you the cellar
where that rising damp emanates from?
I'm off to be a DJ in Lytham St. Anne —

White-faced, still-standing.
Opens the door and says too much:
-The reason I'm leaving is
I lost my wife last year-
Gloomy room. Undone since the 90's,
dark fireplace surround of roses,
dark window frames,
a sunless room. She smiles still, from the frame.
-     I'll leave all this. The TV too.
Don't worry. I have a partner new-

No no no no. It's not the one.
Nor the carpet I wanted to roll on,
in Sugar Lane where something's going on.
Having a laugh at that price,
the leasehold predators circle round.

What in a deep valley possesses you ?

The sparse trees and mossy bank,
moors alight in the distance,
raises your heart from the cul-de-sac of despond,
lifts one side of a smile,
the joker taking hold.
Really? Are you sure?
Do we dare to live a little more,
before we are too old?

Sunday by the Canal

Picture this, Banksy:
she has her make-up,
a pretty face and shiny hair up.
In her hands a cigarette
sends swathes of pollutant up.
It is Sunday morning.
The bank is busy with men
pursuing their solo hobbies,
and women following them.
I want to say - don't bother luv,
a man who wants to fish
deserves to be alone,
there'll be no conversation
and even less attention -
It's the grimace of the lipstick,
the menopausal wife
pretending to enjoy herself
ungainly on her mountain bike.
Determined to be fit,
enjoy themselves so far,
the men are quite oblivious,
the girls don't know who they are.

Winter Wishes

Winter wishes hit like leaves in an autumn breeze,
flying away. Their opaque yellow veil
rains down, turning a house to an impression.
A brilliantine drake breaks the fabric,
nonchalantly swims, shining black and green
in brazen full focus, through and beyond.
Something is magical, like a painting,
sun angled into the misty curtain,
like the poem that suddenly arose,
the faint sense of skirting a dimension,
which holds a message, indecipherable,
written in the sky with smoky clouds.
Walk on with wishes falling all around,
faded, unspoken, on early ground.

Make No Plans

Make no plans,
rather, wander aimlessly
from spire to spire,
or lie on dried grass
by river sallows.
For ye gods
I rumbled you,
I know you do not care,
perched high with your fake black beards
and false hair.
There, in the belfry
is the truth,
for no one receives mercy,
the more deserving, the worse.
Flail if you will,
rail against the inevitable,
it comes down to the same thing.
Make no plans.

Flight of the Swallow

Beware the dark swallows,
that fly their ribboned tails in coloured maelstroms of joy
as you walk slowly to church doors with happy lovers
and stand together above the winding sand trails,
to revel, immersed, in unaccustomed sunshine,
though a black shadow flits in the corner of your eye
and a cloud shaped like the cork screw curls of your friend
glides across the sky.
She waited until the last flame of these memories to die,
leaving you with the beauty and the terror of how it would be:
all at once young, all at once telescoped,
those days of youth folded into bone and rose:
the sled processions of children
under laden snow roofs against the highest blue,
days of parenthood, drunk on sleeplessness in the park:
the slides, the cries, the screams, the giggling life of it all.
And further back still, in college days,
how wise she was, how kind, how motherly and able.
Or days you walked steep streets in summer rains,
standing under pouring drains,
the more to drench your laughing faces,
or partying in her parents' grand red house, the teenage
wildness.
Her smile so gracious. Her voice so soft. Gone now.
Teach me how to die with courage
with the speed of the swallow
flying through the halls of a summer marriage.

Matters of Life and Death

I bought myself a birthday present,
a gadget just for me,
the manual didn't intimidate,
I took it apart to clean.
Whole minutes of pleasure with this,
de-bobbling my cashmere,
so pleasing and so silly,
its industrious whirring.
But I'm not thinking of this.
All the time it is summer,
and I'm walking out of Cambridge,
sandals on the hot pavement,
shuffling towards the botanical garden
with the member's card you bade me use.
It wasn't on my list, but how could I refuse?
Those last messages between us:
me, smiling stupidly from the fountain edge.
And when you could no longer speak,
a sign, a heart
to say you loved the cornflower bed.
The gadget whirrs,
my winter clothes are tidier now.
An occupation that calms cannot
erase the scuffing of my sandaled feet,
my sleeveless dress, the hat I bought
to obey your last wish of me.
And my last image of you:

an easing on of shoes
to show us another garden
in the hospital you could not leave.
The gadget whirrs,
I'm still alive
in trivia and deepening cold.

Into the Shallows

I will wade with you into the shallows where the light ripples,
the bars of sunlight broken by brown waters,
the sand firm beneath our feet. I shall hold your hand.
There will be no more words now as we leave the land.
The pale sky will fall gently down to meet
the jagged rocks and the sea floor.
We shall not stumble. I shall hold your hand.
Should I spy a fluted tiger-shell impaled,
I'll reach for it to feel its miraculous sheen,
lacquered by aeons adrift. Long vacated.
Look! I shall say, holding it out to you in gift.
Only then will the light skies shift.
Only sand will trail from my empty hand.
Far far out in the shallows, alone I shall stand.

A Summer Like No Other

It was a summer like no other:
swallows, bees, golden sandbanks
and butterfly jewelled graves.
The lovers posed on a red bench
and we walked to gardens,
lay in water meadows amongst spires,
as bitterness pulled out of town
across an ocean.
The angels stole a friend.
In the end, we could only collect rainbows
which appeared like promises in our path.
In the end, for there was an end,
we could only seek joy.
Two sides of the sorrow.
It was a summer like no other.

Printed in Great Britain
by Amazon